This book belongs to:

Seasons
Greetings

warm
wishes

Merry
Christmas

Happy Holiday

Sweet
Dreams

best
wishes

Stay
Warm

hohoho

Merry
and
Bright

Believe
in the
Magic
of
Christmas

hello
winter

Jingle
Bells

Enjoy

Time
to Stay
Home
2020

www.ingramcontent.com/pod-product-compliance
Lightning Source LLC
Chambersburg PA
CBHW081428250726
48654CB00013B/1859